12 THINGS EVERY INJURED EMPLOYEE MUST KNOW

First Edition

Robert T. Edens

Attorney at Law

(847) 395-2200

www.robertedenslawoffice.com

Copyright © 2013 by Robert T. Edens

All Rights reserved. No part of this book may be reproduced, stored in a retrieval system, or transmitted by any means, electronic, mechanical, photocopying, recording or otherwise, without written permission from the author.

Printed in The United States of America

Robert T. Edens, P.C.
392 Lake St
Antioch, IL 60002
(847) 395-2200

PREFACE

Hello, my name is Robert "Bob" Edens. I have written this book because employees often do not know their rights after suffering an injury on the job. An employee may worry how they will pay for their medical bills, if they will lose their job due to the injury; how they will provide for their family while they recover, and more. These are just a few of the questions I will answer in this book.

I have represented injured workers for the last 20 years and have seen first-hand how workers' compensation insurance companies try to pay the least possible amount for an employee's injuries.

My goal in writing this book is to provide you with an overview of the laws of Illinois as they pertain to Workers' Compensation and how to navigate the complexities of the claims process you will have to deal with along the way. After reading this book you will know your rights regarding, medical bill reimbursement, temporary total disability payments, permanent disability payments and the other benefits you are entitled to. Furthermore, you will have a better understanding if you require the assistance of an attorney to settle your claim.

Not every case requires the services of an attorney. A minor injury without significant medical treatment can probably be handled without hiring an attorney. However, at the very least you should have an attorney look over any settlement offer before you sign it. Most attorneys, including myself, will offer you a free consultation. I will analyze your individual situation and give you an honest, no obligation evaluation. So please read this book and if you still have questions call me to discuss your case in more detail.

12 THINGS EVERY INJURED EMPLOYEE MUST KNOW

First Edition

Robert T. Edens

Attorney at Law

(847) 395-2200

www.robertedenslawoffice.com

Table of Contents

Introduction To The Workers' Compensation Act

1. **Chapter One:** The Most Common Workplace Injuries

2. **Chapter Two:** What To Do After Your Accident

    1. **Immediate Treatment:** Do not let the fear of repercussions or embarrassment keep you from getting medical attention.
    2. **Reporting:** Illinois law requires that your injury be reported to your employer within 45 days from the date of the injury.
    3. **What and Who Determines if You Qualify For Workers' Compensation?** Any injury that prevents you from doing your full time duties for a prolonged period of time, as determined by your doctor(s) entitles you to Workers' Compensation.
    4. **Obligation to Your Employer:** It is your responsibility to keep your employer apprised of your recovery and your anticipated return to work, based on your doctor's recommendation.

3. **Chapter Three:** Myths & Misconceptions About Workers' Compensation.

    Myth: You can't recover damages for your injuries because it was your fault.
    Myth: You can't recover damages because you are a new employee or your employer doesn't provide this coverage.
    Myth: You can't recover damages because you didn't go to the hospital or doctor right away.
    Myth: You can't recover damages because your injuries relate to a "pre-existing" condition.
    Myth: You can't return to work because your position was eliminated while you were out sick.

4. **Chapter Four:** 12 Things Every Illinois Injured Worker Should Understand About Workers' Compensation.

    1. When Does an Employer/Employee Relationship Exist?
    2. When Does an Injury "Arise Out Of" Employment Exist?
    3. When Does an Injury Occur In The Course of Employment?
    4. What is an Average Weekly Wage (AWW)?
    5. What are Total Temporary Disability Benefits (TTD)

6. When do TDD Benefits Start and Stop?
7. What Medical Benefits are Covered?
8. What Are "Permanent Partial Disability Benefits (PPD)?"
9. What is a "Wage Differential Award?"
10. What is "Permanent Total Disability?"
11. What is "Vocational Rehabilitation?"
12. What are "Death Benefits?"

5. **Chapter Five:** 12 Mistakes That Can Ruin Your Workers' Compensation Case

   Mistake 1: Failing to Act Immediately at the Time of the Accident.
   Mistake 2: Failing to Notify Your Doctor of the Details of Your Work-Place Injury.
   Mistake 3: Falsifying Your Injuries and Symptoms.
   Mistake 4: Failing to Select Your Own Doctor.
   Mistake 5: Failure to Follow Your Doctor's Advice, Orders or Treatment Plan.
   Mistake 6: Failure to Return to Work on Light Duty if Your Doctor Says That You Can.
   Mistake 7: Performing Acts Beyond Your Doctors Restrictions.
   Mistake 8: Getting Caught on Videotape Performing Acts Beyond Your Doctor's Restrictions.
   Mistake 9: Assuming That the Workers' Compensation Adjustor has Correctly Determined Your Average Weekly Wage (AWW).
   Mistake 10: Not Hiring the Right Attorney or Not Hiring an Attorney at All.
   Mistake 11: Failing to Be Honest With Your Attorney.
   Mistake 12: Giving a Recorded Statement or Signing a Medical Release for the Insurance Company.

6. **Chapter Six:** 12 Things You Need to Know About Insurance Companies.

   1. **The Insurance Adjuster is Not on Your Side and is Not Going to Treat You Fairly.**
   2. **You Do Not Have to Give a Recorded Statement.**
   3. **You Do Not Have to Sign a Medical Release or Wage Loss Authorization.**
   4. **The Insurance Company May Not Always Tell You The Truth.**

5. Your Injuries Were Pre-Existing and Not Related to Your Accident.
6. The Insurance Company Does Not Want You to Know the Type of Damages You Are Entitled To.
7. Insurance Companies Do Not Want You to Know, or Learn How to Find Out, What Your Injuries are Actually Worth.
8. The Insurance Company Might Try to Blame You for Your Injuries.
9. The Insurance Company Does Not Want You to Know the Long Term Consequences of Your Injuries.
10. The Insurance Company Does Not Want You to Know What a Third-Party Claim is or if One is Available to You.
11. The Insurance Company Does Not Want You to Know That Accident Victims Receive 2-3 Times More Money With an Attorney.
12. The Insurance Company Will Look for Many Reasons to Deny Your Claim, Hoping You Won't Challenge Them.

7. **Chapter Seven:** Choosing The Right Workers' Compensation Attorney

8. **Chapter Eight:** Preparing Your Workers' Comp Case

Frequently Asked Questions (FAQ's)

Conclusion

INTRODUCTION

In Illinois, when someone is injured on the job they are protected under The Workers' Compensation Act. The Worker's Compensation Act. The Workers' Compensation Act provides the following:

- Paid medical care to cure or relieve injuries.

- Temporary disability pay based on pre-injury wages during the period of time the employee is off of work healing.

- Partial disability pays while the employee is recovering but working lighter than normal duties.

- Approved vocational rehabilitation training if you are no longer able to perform the duties you were doing prior to your injury.

- Permanent partial disability for an employee who sustains a permanent injury or disfigurement but can still work in a different job or field.

- Permanent total disability for an employee who is permanently unable to work due to their injuries.

- Death benefits for surviving dependents if an employee dies as a result of a work related injury or disease.

Many employees fear retaliation for filing a claim for Workers' Compensation. However, employers are required to carry insurance for this very purpose. Therefore an employee often will be dealing with an insurance adjuster and not someone from their company. Occasionally, an employer will be self-insured and I will go into more detail about that in later chapters.

It is important to know that the insurance adjuster has been specifically trained to ask very specific questions, usually in a specific order, regarding your injury and how it occurred. The adjuster may be very pleasant and seem to be genuinely concerned for your well-being and your need for money to pay your bills. In reality the adjuster's main objective is to get you to make a statement, sign documents, and settle your claim for as little as possible, as soon as possible. All this before you have the necessary information to make the correct decisions. These questions can damage your claim at a later date.

After 20 years of experience as a Workers' Compensation attorney, I have seen time and time again the unscrupulous tricks and tactics that the adjusters use. In addition, I have witnessed the many mistakes and erroneous misconceptions made by employees who have been hurt on the job. Thankfully, many people have not been seriously injured and can easily settle things on their own and return to work within a short period of time. However, if you are one of the unfortunate ones who suffer more serious injuries, than this book will answer your questions and give you the insight necessary to level the playing field between you and the insurance company. It will alert you to the tricks and traps the insurance company hopes you fall for. It will provide you with an understanding of your rights and your employer's responsibilities under IL Workers' Compensation Act.

CHAPTER ONE

THE MOST COMMON WORKERPLACE INJURIES

The most common injuries differ from one industry to the next. Obviously the top 10 injuries in a machine shop will differ from those of an office environment. Usually the injuries fall into one of these categories.

1. **Over-Exertion Injuries** - The number one cause for workers' compensation injuries is the overexertion of employee's bodies. These injuries occur from heavy or excessive lifting, pulling, carrying, throwing, or pushing. Many jobs require such work. Even smaller tasks such as carrying copy paper in an office can cause back, leg, shoulder, and other strain injuries. Don't be the hero - feel comfortable asking for help if something is too heavy for you to move or lift.

2. **Slipping/Tripping** - Many workplace accidents occur when employees trip over something or slip on materials left unattended. Even bad weather can instigate this type of injury for workers. Attention to what is going on around them is required of employees. Employers should have safety guidelines to ensure spills are promptly cleaned and no debris is present which can be dangerous.

3. **Falling from Heights** - These injuries can occur due to faulty equipment or falling off a ladder or scaffolding. Harnesses and protective gear are necessary to prevent more serious injuries. Also, the equipment needs to be checked and replaced regularly to prevent injury. The

Chapter One

workplace environment needs to be secure and regularly checked for equipment and structural problems.

4. **Reactive Injuries** – A reaction by an employee to a situation, such as jumping out of the way of a falling object or pulling back when startled can cause muscle injuries & tears, body trauma, and a variety of other medical issues. These incidents are not always avoidable or foreseeable so it is important to remind employees to stay alert and aware of their surroundings.

5. **Falling Objects**- These injuries occur when something falls from above and strikes a part of the body. A common cause of this is when an employee reaches overhead to get something from a higher area. Head injuries are a common result of this type of accident. Proper work gear and attention to ones surroundings can keep these injuries to a minimum.

6. **Walking Into Objects** – As odd as this sounds, there are many reported injuries caused by employees walking into objects within their environment. Head, knee, ankle, neck, and foot injuries are common results of these walking type injuries. An employee's attention to their surroundings and a focus on keeping the work environment free from hazards are key to preventing these types of injuries.

7. **Vehicle Accidents** -Workers who drive as part of their job duties can be injured in an auto accident, some of which can be fatal. As a driver, an employee has a responsibility to follow protocols and safety measures put in place by the employer which often includes not talking on a cell phone or texting while operating the vehicle.

The Most Common Workplace Injuries

8. **Machinery Injuries** - Workers using and working around heavy equipment and machinery are susceptible to getting caught in the moving parts of the device. Clothing, shoes, fingers, and hair are common items that can easily get caught or compressed by everyday equipment during normal operation. Protective equipment and attention to personal details are necessary to avoid these incidents.

9. **Repetitive Motion Injuries** - Carpal tunnel syndrome is one of the most common injuries and is caused by the continuous, repeated motion used to perform ones job. Factory workers or those who do a tremendous amount of typing are frequent sufferers of carpal tunnel syndrome.

10. **Violent Acts** - These acts occur when an employee gets angry at his/her co-workers, management, or anyone they perceive as "wronging" them in some way. Fortunately, this is the least occurring of our top 10 injuries. Preventative education and employee training to spot and report suspicious behaviors keep incidents from being exacerbated. If you suspect something or are being provoked by a co-worker, talk to your manager or Human Resources Department. Don't let something get out of control.

If you have experienced any of the above injuries during your workday, it is important to protect your potential workers' compensation claim. We are here to help you figure out the best course of action for your claim. Contact our office today by calling toll free 855-760-6746 or use our online form at RobertEdensLawOffice.com. We'll give you a free, honest, evaluation of your case and explain to you

Chapter One

*what your options are. The call is **FREE**, the advice may be priceless.*

CHAPTER TWO

What To Do After Your Accident

The Workers' Compensation Act places several obligations on the injured employee and the employer after an injury occurs on the job. A few of these obligations are discussed below.

1. **Immediate Treatment:** Do not let the fear of repercussions or embarrassment keep you from getting medical attention. Ultimately, this can have great bearing on the outcome of your worker's compensation claim. Aside from it being your legal responsibility to report your injury to your employer, you owe it to yourself to get medical attention, even if you don't think you are seriously injured. Once the adrenaline wears off, you may feel worse then you did right after your accident. Also, there can be injuries that would otherwise not be detected until a later date if you do not get treatment.

2. **Reporting:** Illinois law requires that your injury be reported to your employer within 45 days from the date of the injury. It is not always readily apparent that you have suffered an injury at the time of the accident or the extent of your injuries so the law allows sufficient time after the occurrence for any latent injuries to surface.

3. **What and Who Determines if You Qualify For Workers' Compensation?** Any injury that prevents you from doing your full time duties for a prolonged period of time, as determined by your doctor(s), entitles you to medical and compensation benefits. Your employer can't fire you or insist you return to work unless your doctor clears you to return to work, full-time, part-time or light duty. In many cases your doctor will put restrictions on the tasks

Chapter Two

you can perform. Examples include no lifting over 10 pounds, no bending, and no standing over one hour, to name a few. In these cases your employer may either find another job for you to do or tell you to stay at home until your restrictions are lifted. Problems in this area often arise. There are specific rules that apply, and if this is your situation, it would be wise to consult an attorney to discuss the specific details of your case.

4. **Obligation to Your Employer:** It is your responsibility to keep your employer apprised of your recovery and your anticipated return to work date. In almost all instances your employer will not allow you to return to work without documentation from your doctor stating that you are allowed to return to work and in what capacity. If the adjuster requests that you go to see their doctor for an "independent medical review," you are required to comply. **Understand this medical review is anything but independent. It is an attempt by the adjuster to justify the discontinuance of your benefits and reduce the amount of your permanency award. If the adjuster requests that you go to such an exam, it is highly recommended that you consult an attorney beforehand.**

If you, or someone you love has been injured on the job and the adjuster is asking that you see their doctor, call Bob, **toll free** at 855-760-6746 or use our online form at RobertEdensLawOffice.com. The call is free, the advice may be priceless!

CHAPTER THREE

MYTHS & MISCONCEPTIONS ABOUT WORKERS' COMPENSATION CASES

If you have been involved in a work-related injury you will only get one chance to get the compensation you deserve. Therefore, it is important that you separate fact from fiction.

Myth: You can't recover for your injuries because you were at fault.

Truth: Even if your injury was your own fault you are still entitled to full benefits under The Workers' Compensation Act. So long as your injury occurred at work, or in the course of performing your duties and there were no special circumstances that would preclude recovery, you are entitled to certain benefits.

Myth: You can't recover because there are no witnesses to the accident.

Truth: In many cases there won't be any witnesses to your accident. However, that has little bearing on your ability to collect benefits. Again, as long as you were hurt at work or during the course of performing your duties then you are entitled to receive benefits. It is important to remember that it is your obligation to notify your employer as soon as possible about your injuries.

Myth: You can't recover damages because you are a new employee or your employer does not provide this coverage.

Truth: This is a myth that some employers might like you to believe. The fact is your employer is required by law to carry workers compensation insurance and not doing so may result in fines and subject the employer to liability.

Chapter Three

If your employer provided you with a handbook when you were hired, it is a good idea to give a copy to your attorney. There will usually be a section specifically detailing what to do if you've been injured at work.

Myth: You can't recover because you didn't go to the hospital or doctor right away.

Truth: Injuries aren't always immediately evident. An employee may feel fine immediately after the incident but a serious injury may develop later. While it is advised you seek medical attention as soon as possible after an accident, it does not automatically prevent you from bringing a worker's compensation claim for injuries caused by the accident.

Myth: You can't recover because your injuries relate to a "pre-existing" condition.

Truth: An accident can often further injuries in an area that is already weakened by a prior condition. This is most common in back, shoulder, and knee injuries. An insurance company will try to use the fact that you received treatment to the same area to their advantage. For example: A person might have a previous shoulder injury, but as a result of *this* accident, they may now have a permanent injury and require surgery. An experienced attorney will have encountered this issue on many prior occasions and can aggressively challenge the insurance company's allegations. Therefore, it is important to tell your physician, as well as your attorney, about any prior injuries as the insurance adjuster will eagerly argue that you were intentionally being deceptive to collect money for a pre-existing injury when you had no intention.

Myth: You can't return to work because your position was eliminated while you were out sick.

Myths & Misconceptions About Workers Compensation Cases

Truth: Your employer does not have to hold your particular position open but they do have to place you in a position at the same salary you were receiving at the time of your accident.

If you have been told one or more of these myths, especially by an insurance company, you can easily find out the truth by consulting an experienced attorney who handles workers' compensation cases and will evaluate the unique circumstances of your individual accident.

If you are unsure what your rights are after being injured on the job, call Bob, toll free, at 855-760-6746 for a **FREE**, honest, evaluation. The call is free, the advice may be

CHAPTER FOUR

12 THINGS EVERY ILLINOIS INJURED WORKER SHOULD UNDERSTAND ABOUT WORKERS' COMPENSATION

1. **When Does an Employer/Employee Relationship Exist?**

   A stipulation of the Illinois Workers' Compensation Law is that for an injured worker to receive benefits there must be an employer/employee relationship between the parties. In most cases this is not an issue. However, in some cases an employer may claim that the injured worker is an independent contractor.

   When there is a question regarding the employer/employee relationship the Workers' Compensation Commission will examine the relationship and make a determination. There isn't one single factor that will determine the outcome. Factors including the right to control the work, the method of payment, the right to discharge, the skill required to perform the work, and whether the employer furnish the tools, materials or equipment. The right to control the work is the single most important factor in determining whether or not an employer/employee relationship exists.

   a. **What Benefits Does the Act Provide?**

      When an employee is injured on the job, he/she can only recover damages from their employer under the Worker's Compensation Act. An injured worker may not sue his/her employer in Circuit Court.

Chapter Four

> However, if a third party was at fault for the employees injuries, the employee will have a "cause of action" against the at fault individual for the company. This is common in vehicle accident cases.

Generally speaking, the Illinois Workers' Compensation Act provides the following benefits:

- <u>Temporary Total Disability (T.T.D.) Benefits:</u> You are entitled to recover 66% of your average weekly wage during the entire time you are unable to work as a result of the work-related injury.

- <u>Medical Expenses:</u> You are entitled to recover your medical expenses that you incur and that are reasonably certain to be incurred in the future as a result of the injury. You are entitled to choose your own doctor and go to any specialist he refers you to. The insurance company is required to pay for the specialist's medical bills.

- <u>Permanent Partial Disability (P.P.D.) Benefits:</u> The injured employee is entitled to a permanent disability benefit based on the part of the body injured and the nature, and degree of the injury. The rate for determining the benefit is 60% of the average gross wages times the number of weeks that the injury is determined to disable the employee. This is the amount from which your attorney is paid his 20% fee. Additionally, this is the amount the insurance company will argue over most.

Unlike an automobile accident when the plaintiff is entitled to other benefits above and beyond, in a workers' compensation case, the injured worker is limited to the above benefits because they do not have to prove another person or entity was at fault, only that his injury arose out of and was in the course of his employment. There are other benefits under the Act, so if you were severely injured it is highly recommended that you consult an attorney to protect your rights.

It is important that you are aware of these benefits because it is not uncommon for the insurance company to offer you a lesser amount then you deserve. Insurance companies are in the business of making money. The way they do that is by collecting premiums and not paying claims.

b. **What is a Statutory Employer?**

The Illinois Workers' Compensation Act provides benefits not only to employees, but also to the employees of sub-contractors who directly or indirectly perform any work. This portion of the Act is important because it benefits an injured worker who is employed by a sub-contractor who does not have worker's compensation insurance of their own or does not have the assets to pay benefits that the injured worker is entitled to. If you were injured and your employer did not have worker's compensation but there was a general contractor on the job, you can file what is known as "an application for adjustment" claim against your employer and the general contractor who becomes the "statutory" employer. The statutory employer is then responsible for paying your benefits. After those benefits are paid and your case is closed, the statutory employer has the right to sue your employer for reimbursement.

c. **What Notice Must Be Given to the Employer?**

Chapter Four

The Act requires that an injured employee give the employer notice of the injury within 45 days from the date the injury occurred. This notice must be given to a supervisor, human resource manager or any other member of the management team. This notice can be given orally or in writing. If it is oral the employer will usually write up the details themselves based on the employee's account.

Again, this is why I stated previously that you should write down everything you can remember about the accident and/or your injuries before you forget. Failure to notify the employer within the 45 day time period will be something the insurance company will use to avoid paying you benefits. Within 3 years from the date of the accident or 2 years after the last payment of benefits has been made. This is the statutory time frame allowed. Once it passes you will be forever barred from receiving further benefits.

2. **When Does an Injury "Arise Out Of" Employment?"**

The injury must happen when an employee performs work and not on a personal errand. Therefore, the statement "arising out of employment" simply means that the employee's injuries are traceable to a specific time, place and cause, all of which are related to their employment.

Not all injuries which happen during work are covered by the Act. The Act does not cover an injury just because it happened at work. For example, if an employee trips while walking down the hall, without any reason or defect in the flooring, then this is not compensable under the Act because the worker was not at any more risk than the general public would be. However, if an employee was walking down the hall while carrying a large box of work related materials and tripped, then this could be sufficient to qualify for benefits. If you have questions about your particular situation then please speak to an experienced attorney who can advise you properly. **Don't attempt to handle this on your own. If you are being denied benefits call an experienced attorney for advice .**

There are a handful of states that allow benefits for an injury just because it occurs during work hours, regardless if the risk was personal but Illinois is not one of these states.

a. <u>**Fighting at the Work-place**</u>

A fight between co-workers' regarding performance of work is entitled to benefits under the Act. However, the aggressor is not entitled to benefits if they are hurt during the fight. If a fight breaks out due to personal reasons then neither party is entitled to benefits. An example would be, if a co-worker attacks an employee because he or she suspects them of keying their car in the parking lot, then any claim arising out of this situation would be denied. An exception occurs if you were an innocent bystander who was injured during the course of this fight.

b. <u>**Recreational Activities**</u>

An employee may be covered under the Act during recreational activities but each case is qualified under specific facts. For example, an employee that is injured while playing on a company's softball team may qualify for benefits if the employer supplied uniforms, paid any team fees and/or allowed time off with pay for practice and the games. Another example is if an injury occurs at a company picnic. If the employer required attendance at the company picnic then that injury would qualify for benefits under the Act. If the employee's attendance at the company picnic is voluntary, and the employee has the option of attending the company picnic or having the day off, an injury occurring at that company picnic will generally be denied benefits.

c. **Intoxicated Employee**

In general, an employee who gets injured on the job while intoxicated will still qualify for benefits under the Act. However, there is an exemption if the employer can show that the employee was so severely intoxicated that he/she was unable to perform their job. Failure to pass a field sobriety test, being charged with a DUI or having a blood alcohol level above the legal limit will not automatically deny an injured worker benefits. Of course, the employer is going to argue that if the employee was legally intoxicated at the time of the injury then the injury didn't "arise out of employment." Again, the general rule of thumb is that alcohol or drug use will not bar benefits under the Act.

3. **When Does an Injury Occur "In the Course of" Employment?**

An injury must also happen during the course of employment. This means either at the physical location or during work duties that might be at another location as part of the employees overall responsibilities.

Generally, commuting to and from work are not covered by the Act. However, if you are running a special errand for the company or if the employer is paying your travel expenses to and from work then you are entitled to benefits.

Many cases involving this question surround injuries which happen in the parking lot. In the event a worker is injured in a parking lot that is owned by the employer, or if the employer requires employees to park in a certain area, generally an injury will be covered under the Act.

As you have read, determining a case's eligibility under the Act is very fact-specific and it is beneficial to have an experienced worker's compensation attorney to avoid losing a case, or falling victim to the hidden dangers and pitfalls the insurance carrier will commonly use to trip up the injured worker to avoid paying out any benefits.

4. **What is The Average Weekly Wage?**

The Average Weekly Wage, also known as AWW, is the foundation which most benefits are determined including Temporary Total Disability (TTD) and Partial Permanent Disability (PPD) benefits. The AWW is determined by averaging a worker's pay for the 52 weeks preceding the injury. While this seems straight forward, it is common for claims adjusters, and defense attorneys working for the insurance companies, to fail to include overtime, holiday/vacation or incentive pay when calculating benefits. The Act states that overtime should be included in the average weekly wage computation so long as the overtime is mandatory and occurs on a regular basis. Failing to hire an experienced workers' compensation attorney can jeopardize an employee's right to receive the full pay they are entitled to. It is crucial that you consult an experienced attorney to determine if the average weekly wage is calculated correctly and challenge an adjuster or insurance company if the AWW is incorrect.

a. **Bonuses/Fringe Benefits**

The Act specifically excludes bonuses and fringe benefits in the calculation of the AWW. The reason for the exclusion is that "bonuses" are not based on specific work performed by an employee.

Chapter Four

While bonuses are not payable under the Act, incentive pay is included in the AWW calculation so long as the employer has included the incentive pay in the employee's regular wage statements. Again, unscrupulous adjusters will try to say that incentive pay was actually a bonus but an experienced attorney will ensure that your pay is calculated correctly.

b. **Employees Who Have a Second Job**

Many employees do not realize that if they have a second job which the employer knows about, the wages of the second job are added to the employee's regular wage to calculate his average weekly wage. This will result in the injured employee receiving additional money for the claim. It is not likely that an insurance adjuster will include a second job pay in the average weekly wage calculation for an injured employee. Insurance companies hire experienced worker's compensation defense attorneys, and pay them large fees to defend worker's compensation claims. There have been many lawsuits and court cases surrounding the calculation of an injured worker's AWW Again, this is why it can be very beneficial to retain an experienced worker's compensation attorney who will be on your side and will stand up to the adjuster and big insurance companies.

5. **How Are Temporary Total Disability Benefits (TTD) Calculated?**

The TTD benefits are payment to an injured worker for the time that he or she is off from work recovering from their injuries. These benefits are calculated at two-thirds of an injured worker's average weekly wage. The higher a person's AWW, the higher his TTD benefit check, thus it is important to make sure that there is an appropriate average weekly wage calculation.

The Act has set both a maximum and minimum TTD benefit. The current maximum TTD benefit is $1,178.48 per week and the current minimum TTD benefit is $200.00 per week for a non-married employee. Below are minimum TTD benefits based on the injured worker's marital status and number of children.

Married:	$230.00
Married, 1 child:	$260.00
Married, 2 children:	$290.00
Married, 3+ children:	$300.00

If an injured worker was working only part-time and his average weekly wage was less than the minimum, then his entire average weekly wage will be used as the TTD benefits.

6. When Do TTD Benefits Start and Stop?

TTD benefits start to accrue the day after an injured worker is unable to return to work as a result of his work-related injury. However, if the injured worker is able to return to work within 14 days of getting the injury then they will only be paid from the 3rd day to the 14th day. It is only when the worker is off more than 14 days that the Act requires the insurance carrier to pay the TTD benefits from the first day after the injury occurred.

Temporary Total Disability (TDD) payments stop when the injured employee has returned to work without restrictions.

a. **Defense Medical Exam**

Chapter Four

Under the Act the employer has the right to require the injured employee to be examined by their own physician. This is sometimes referred to as an "independent medical exam." However, it is anything but independent. These doctors work for the employer. The employer is required to pay any traveling expenses to and from the defense medical examination and is required to pay any wages if the defense medical examination is scheduled and conducted during a time when the injured worker is usually at work. It is important that you realize that TTD benefits **can be terminated and/or temporarily suspended if the employee refuses to submit to a medical examination requested by the employer.**

It is common for the insurance company to exercise this right and use it to their advantage. Often they will schedule this examination with very little notice, hoping the injured worker will not show up, so they can suspend the worker's TTD benefits. This can be a real hardship for the worker and his or her family.

If an employer or worker's compensation insurance company does suspend TTD benefits, the employee has the right to file an emergency petition to prove to the arbitrator that the employee is still entitled to benefits under the Act. The petition requires 15-day notice to the employer prior to the hearing and a current doctor's note stating that the injured worker is unable to return to work as a result of his work-related injury. The doctor's note should include the basis of the doctor's opinion why the injured worker is unable to return to work.

b. **Maintenance Benefits**

The Act also provides that in certain cases of a severe injury an injured worker, after he reaches maximum medical improvement, is entitled to receive

12 Mistakes That Can Ruin Your Workers' Compensation Case

"maintenance" benefits if he is unable to return to work at his former position. During this time the worker might also undergo vocational rehabilitation training. The maintenance benefit is paid at the same rate as the previous TTD benefits. See the section on Vocational Rehabilitation for further explanation.

c. **Overpayment of TTD Benefits**

While rare, there are occasions when an injured worker is accidently overpaid under the Act and the insurance companies will fight hard to get repayment of that money. They can take their case to an appellate court which can order repayment for the extra money or can issue a credit against any permanency award or PPD benefit the worker may receive.

7. **What Medical Benefits are Covered?**

An employer is required to pay for all the medical bills (associated with the work injury only) incurred by an injured worker during his or her recovery time. The law also requires that the employer continue paying for medical bills for the rest of the employee's life. Despite this, in most cases the injured worker will settle the case and waive any right to future benefits.

By signing a settlement contract the injured worker can't come back at a later date and prove that his future medical treatment and care was causally related to the original work injury. This is why it is important that your medical care providers have fully treated your current injuries. Only after you have been fully treated should you settle your workers' compensation claim.

a. **The Right to Choose Your Own Doctor**

Chapter Four

Many injured employees are surprised to find out that they have the right to select the doctor of their choice. All too often workers' defer to their employer, assuming they have to see the company doctor, if there is one. However, not every company doctor has the best interest of the patient in mind when it comes to medical treatment and return to work issues.

If your employer insists that you need to be seen or treated by the company doctor consider seeking the advice of an experienced workers' compensation attorney. Bob offers a FREE, honest, no obligation consultation and will even take your case on a contingency basis if it meets the necessary criteria. Call toll free at **855-760-6746.** The call is free, the advice might be priceless.

b. **Two (2) Doctor Rule**

Not only does the injured worker have the absolute right to choose their own physician for their medical treatment resulting from a work injury, the injured worker is entitled to a second opinion. In addition, the worker may receive additional treatment by any referred physician from either of the initial doctors. It is the employer's responsibility to pay for these visits and any additional treatment recommended.

c. **Defense Medical Exam**

As stated prior, since the injured employee has the right to choose his own treating physicians, the law provides the employer the right to have the injured employee examined by a physician of their choice. This is known as the Section 12 Exam, which is a defense medical exam. The injured employee is required by the Act to be examined by the defense medical examiner. Failure to submit to the exam is grounds to cut off your rights to receive TTD benefits.

Attorney Robert Edens, P.C. recommends to all his clients required to undergo a Section 12 defense medical exam to wear a watch and document exactly how long the defense medical examining doctor actually examines them as opposed to how long they were in the waiting room and/or spoke to the defense medical examiner's nurse and note exactly what tests he performs and any questions that were asked. Then after the exam to make notes of all the facts so they can be recalled later.

d. **Continued Medical Benefits**

Even after an injured employee reaches his or her Maximum Medical Improvement (MMI) and has returned to work full duty without restrictions, they may be entitled to further benefits. This usually occurs where an injured employee's condition will not improve despite all the medical treatment they have received to date and they are in need of on-going pain relief expenses.

8. What Are Permanent Partial Disability Benefits (PPD)?

The permanent partial disability (PPD) benefits are the amount of money the injured employee receives after he recovers from his work-related injury. The Act has assigned a specific number of weeks of compensation for injuries to various body parts. The current maximum amount of weeks for each body part is as follows:

Arm – 253

Chapter Four

Leg – 215

Hand – 205

Foot – 167

Big Toe – 38

All 10 Toes – 13

Thumb – 76

Index Finger – 43

Middle Finger – 38

Ring Finger - 27

Little Finger – 22

Whole Person – 500

However, it is not as straight forward as the above figures. Only an experienced workers' compensation attorney will fight for your right to collect the benefits you deserve. The insurance company and their defense attorneys will <u>always</u> underestimate the percentage of disability that the injured employee is entitled to despite the calculation for the PPD benefit being very simple.

To calculate the proper PPD payment, you multiply the average weekly wage (AWW) by 60%, then you take that number and multiply it by the percentage loss for each specific body part that was injured on the job. For example, if the average weekly wage is $500 and the employee lost 75% use of one of their arms then the calculation is as follows:

$500 x 60% = $300 then take

$300 x 75% = $225 to arrive at $225 per week

There is a maximum PPD rate of $636.15 per week or 60% of $1060. Any worker having an average weekly wage of over $1060.00 per week or $55,133.00 per year is at the maximum.

a. **Disfigurement**

Disfigurement, commonly known as scarring, carries a maximum of 150 weeks of benefits. For the scarring, to be compensable, it must be serious and permanent to the hands, face, head, neck, arm, leg below the knee, or chest above the sternum. The disfigurement benefit is calculated on a case-by-case basis and can't be settled until six months have passed since the injury. To obtain the maximum benefit possible under the Act, a disfigured injured worker should consult an experienced worker's compensation attorney to determine the value of that case.

PPD Benefits **don't** include the following:

1. Past pain and suffering.
2. Future pain and suffering.
3. Loss of a normal life.
4. Temporary aggravations of a condition.
5. An injury or scar that completely disappears.
6. Risk of future injury.

9. What is a Wage Differential Award?

A wage differential is an award made to the injured worker when he or she is unable to return to their former position and the job they are able to perform pays less than their past earnings. If an injured worker qualifies for a wage differential award, the award is generally substantial

Chapter Four

because, pursuant to the Act, the injured worker is entitled to wage differential benefits for the remainder of his natural life, not just his working life.

The wage differential is calculated by taking 66.3% of the difference between the average weekly wage and what the worker currently earns in the new lower paying position. This benefit is paid weekly for life if the case is won at trial. If the case is going to be settled, the attorneys will estimate the injured worker's life expectancy and multiply the weekly benefit times the life expectancy of the injured worker. That figure is then multiplied by a discount rate. In a wage differential case, the lower the discount rate is, the higher the money award is to the injured worker. Generally, a wage differential award greatly exceeds any specific body part PPD award.

You can be sure that neither the workers' compensation adjuster nor the workers' compensation defense attorney will tell you that you have a wage differential case. They will attempt to settle your case on a loss of use basis, in an effort to save the insurance company money.

10. What is a **Permanent Total Disability Benefit?**

If an injured worker is found to be permanently and totally disabled they are entitled to receive two-thirds of their average weekly wage for the rest of their life, subject to the statutory maximums and minimums allowed.

In accordance with the Act there are two types of Permanent Total Disability (PTD) awards. The first is when the injured worker is completely and permanently disabled as a result of their injury; completely incapable of work. The second form is where there is a specific case of loss to both hands, both arms, both feet, both legs, both eyes, or any combination of the two. This is generally referred to as the "statutory permanent total" and has been the basis of many lawsuits and litigation regarding what constitutes a complete Permanent Total Disability. The Supreme Court of Illinois has held that an employee is totally and permanently disabled when he is "unable to make some contribution to the workforce sufficient to justify the payment of wages". While the injured worker may be able to perform some intermittent work they are unable to earn a living because the work they can perform is so limited that no reasonable, stable employment exists in the job market.

There are two types of Permanent Total Disability cases that are not classified as statutory:

    a.   Workers that are "obviously unemployable," and
    b.   Odd lot category workers.

An odd lot on a total disability case is when an injured worker has been unsuccessful in finding work even after a diligent effort has been made, or because of their age, condition, training, education and experience, he is unfit to perform any but the most menial tasks for which no stable employment market exists. If the injured worker is able to show either of the two, the burden shifts to the employer to prove that a stable employment market does exists and regular and continuous work is available.

Obviously, a Permanent Total Disability case is a complicated and difficult subject with too many hidden dangers and pitfalls. An experienced workers' compensation attorney is prepared to skillfully challenge the arguments the insurance company will try to use to deny your claim.

11. What is Vocational Rehabilitation?

If an injured worker is unable to perform the same duties that they were able to prior to the injury then the Act

Chapter Four

requires an employer to pay for vocational rehabilitation training. Additionally, during the time of re-training, the employer is required to pay "maintenance benefits" which are calculated at the same two thirds of the average weekly wage, essentially the same amount as the rate of the TTD benefits. Maintenance benefits are to be paid the entire time the injured worker is undergoing vocational rehabilitation training.

To qualify for vocational rehabilitation benefits, the work injury must have caused a reduction in the employee's earning power. Evidence must also exist demonstrating that vocational rehabilitation will increase the injured worker's earning capacity and the employee is likely to obtain employment upon completion of the vocational rehabilitation. If the injured worker qualifies for vocational rehabilitation, a vocational rehabilitation plan should be filed with the Illinois Workers' Compensation Commission. The employer is responsible for paying for all the treatment, instruction and training necessary for the physical, mental and vocational rehabilitation of the employee including all maintenance costs and expenses.

Since vocational rehabilitation cases are expensive, insurance companies spend lots of effort, energy and money defending against them. These cases are very complex and it is advisable to see an attorney to help you navigate the complexities of these types of cases.

12. **What are Death Benefits?**

In the event an employee dies due to an accident or workplace injury the surviving spouse, or minor child, is entitled to death benefits at two-thirds of the worker's average weekly wage. The death benefit to the surviving spouse or minor child is payable for 25 years or $250,000.00, whichever is greater. Burial expenses are also covered at a current benefit of $8,000.00 to the surviving spouse, dependent or to the actual person incurring the expense.

If the surviving spouse remarries and there are not any surviving minor children at the time of the remarriage who were entitled to compensation benefits under the Act, the surviving spouse shall be paid a lump sum equal to two years compensation benefits and all further rights of the spouse shall terminate and no further benefits may be collected.

CHAPTER FIVE

12 MISTAKES THAT CAN RUIN YOUR WORKERS' COMPENSATION CASE

Mistake 1: Failing to Act Immediately at the Time of the Accident.

At the time of an accident or injury a worker may be embarrassed, dazed or disoriented. They may not be thinking as clearly as they normally would, even if they have no outward appearance of injuries.

Certain things should be done at the time of the accident including remaining calm. If other workers' witness an employee getting injured, they most likely will offer aid and assistance to the worker and will have their own version of events. However, your version of the events leading up to and after the accident will be vital to your case.

As soon as possible you should document everything you can remember about your accident including, what you were doing prior to the accident occurring, at the moment of the accident and immediately after the accident; make note of anything that was said by you, your co-workers, and emergency personnel. Details you may think are insignificant can prove to be critical to your claim at a later date. The more time that passes after an accident, the more details will be forgotten. How many times do we say to ourselves, "I should have written it down?" It is for this very reason you need to write down the details before they slip from your memory.

A record should be kept of the nature and extent of all injuries and any pain or symptoms you may be having as a result of your injuries. A good method to accomplish this is to purchase a separate calendar to keep track of your doctor's visits and symptoms. It can be a wall or pocket

Chapter Five

calendar, or something as simple as a print out from your computer.

Finally, make sure to keep copies of everything, including all costs associated with the injury. Those costs may include loss of wages, travel to and from doctors appointments, special services, or necessary after care. Also, get copies of all of your doctor's records, x-ray, MRI or CT results and lab reports *every time* you have an appointment. **This can't be stressed enough**. It will save enormous amounts of time, energy, and expense rather than you or your attorney having to do it at a later date. Keep these and the corresponding medical bills together in a folder or large binder.

Mistake 2: Failing to Inform Your Doctor of the Details of Your Work-Place Injury.

It is important to tell your doctor everything you can about the details of your injuries from this accident and any prior injuries to the same part of your body, also known as "pre-existing" conditions. Generally when people are asked "how are you?'" they politely respond "fine." However, when your doctor asks this question, he or she really *does* want to know how you're feeling, not merely exchanging pleasantries. Be honest with your doctor about all of your symptoms, including changing and evolving symptoms.

If you are feeling better, let your doctor know. It is imperative that you do not embellish your injuries as discussed below.

Mistake 3: Falsifying Your Injuries and Symptoms.

Sometimes people feel the need to embellish their symptoms or fabricate additional injuries in an effort to strengthen their claim. Unknowingly to you, doctors will generally perform several tests during your examination to determine if you are exaggerating your injuries. While this might be tempting, it can also be the end of your workers' compensation case. If a doctor believes you are embellishing your symptoms to bolster your claim they will note the term "malingerer" (which means faking or exaggerating injuries) in your medical records and that can destroy your case. This is a bad idea as it can actually devalue your claim, or dismiss it altogether. Additionally, insurance fraud is illegal; the risk is too great and the benefit too little.

Mistake 4: Failing to Select Your Own Doctor.

This is a mistake that an injured worker may not even be aware they are making. Larger companies often have doctors on staff or retainer for employee injuries. The injured employee may wrongly assume that they have to see and be treated by the company doctor, and frankly I believe that is exactly what these larger companies want you to believe. In fact, the Act protects the injured employee's right to see and be treated by the doctor of their choice, as well as, any other medical provider the primary physician recommends. In addition, the injured worker is entitled to a second opinion, as well as any services or tests these secondary doctors recommend as part of their overall treatment plan.

Mistake 5: Failure to Follow Your Doctor's Advice, Orders or Treatment Plan.

Another way your claim can be diminished or denied is by not following your doctor's treatment plan or advice. If your doctor orders follow-up tests or physical therapy, it is extremely important that you follow up on everything, even if you are feeling better. Patients often think of their treatment like aspirin – take two and you will feel better. When they feel better they wrongfully assume they can discontinue care. However, if your injuries could be treated

Chapter Five

this way you wouldn't need to file a workers' compensation claim. Symptoms often diminish during treatment but can rapidly return, or even worsen, if treatment is discontinued. Failing to follow your doctor's advice is the easiest way for the insurance company to argue that your injuries are not as serious as you are making them out to be.

Contrary to exaggerating your injuries, you should tell your doctor everything about your injuries. About all symptoms you are experiencing, no matter how minor, as well as any prior injuries you had before the accident. Many clients wrongfully believe if their injuries were pre-existing they have no claim.

Mistake 6: Failure to Return to Work on Light Duty if Your Doctor Says that You Can.

Your doctor may advise you to go back to work with lesser responsibilities then you had prior to your accident. Even if it seems like a job you are overqualified for or beneath you, failing to return to work when your doctor states you can will only bolster the employer's defense that you really do not want to get back to work. If you honestly do not think you can perform the duties being asked of you, discuss your concerns with your doctor. If your doctor still feels you can do what is being asked of you, and then return to work and document any pain, discomfort, uneasiness or other symptoms that arise so you can follow up with your doctor and make any revisions to your duties as necessary.

Mistake 7: Performing Acts Beyond Your Doctors Restrictions.

Even when people are sick or injured they are tempted to do more than what they should. We live in a world when now is not soon enough and it is often easier to do something ourselves then wait for help or assistance. As tempting as it might be to carry in that bag of groceries, walk down a long driveway to get the package you are expecting from the mailbox, etc. wait for the necessary help. Nothing is as important as your health and returning to your pre-injury state.

Mistake 8: Getting Caught on Videotape Performing Acts Beyond Your Doctor's Restrictions.

This is the greatest mistake an injured worker can make. As stated above, it is extremely tempting to do things for one's self, especially when living alone. However, it is the one time when you do venture down the driveway to get that heavy package out of the mailbox, or carry in that bag of groceries, when you are caught in the act by a zealous insurance adjuster who has sent out a private investigator for the sole purpose of discrediting the injured worker.

Mistake 9: Assuming That the Workers' Compensation Adjustor Has Correctly Determined Your Average Weekly Wage (AWW).

As stated prior, it is not uncommon for the adjustor to exclude overtime hours, holiday/vacation pay or incentives when calculating the average weekly wage of an injured employee. By following the formula set forth in chapter four you can easily figure out your own Average Weekly Wage just by adding up **all** your pay, with the exception of bonuses (which is different than incentive pay or commission) for the 52 weeks prior to the injury and taking this total pay and divide by 52. The resulting number is the AWW. **If you have any questions or need help calculating your average weekly wage contact Bob toll free at 855-760-6746. The call is free, the advice might be priceless.**

Mistake 10: Not Hiring the Right Attorney or Not Hiring an Attorney at All.

Chapter Five

No matter how nice an insurance adjuster appears to be, do not believe he has your best interests at heart. They work for the employer's insurance company. The adjuster's job is to pay you the least amount of benefits and that is in the <u>best interest of his or her employer.</u> This is not to say that all employer's or their insurance companies, are out to intentionally deceive people. In some cases injuries that do not present long term health consequences do not require any further action on your part. Only you can decide. The decision should be made with all the facts considered and only after all of your treatment is completed or a treatment plan has been outlined going forward. An experienced Workers' Compensation attorney will be able to discuss these facts, pointing out anything that you may not have even considered. An adept workers' compensation attorney will evaluate any proposed settlement objectively and make any appropriate recommendations before you sign or agree to anything.

Perhaps the most critical factor to receiving a favorable settlement outcome for your work-place injuries is the attorney you select to represent you. Just like doctors that specialize in a particular field of medicine, attorneys specialize in specific practice areas. For the best possible outcome in your workers' compensation case, you should hire an experienced attorney that has a proven record of success in various types of work-place injury claims.

Mistake 11: Failing to Be Honest With Your Attorney.

It is imperative that you disclose everything that could be relevant to your case with your attorney. This includes: prior injuries, current medical conditions, any doctor's care you are under, prior legal issues, financial issues, alcohol or chemical use, employment history, or anything your employer's insurance company can use to discredit you. It is important to remember your attorney is fighting for you and

12 Mistakes That Can Ruin Your Workers' Compensation Case

can't defend something he/she is not even aware of.

In today's day and age it is difficult to keep things confidential. With a few keystrokes anyone can access public information online about you through the FOIA (Freedom of Information Act) including prior arrests, property transactions, bankruptcy, prior and pending lawsuits, and all court proceedings. With a little foresight and savvy, an insurance investigator can track your activities and whereabouts through social media sites. People unsuspectingly post details and pictures online that can devalue or jeopardize their entire claim. You can be sure the insurance companies will have someone checking, at least intermittently, to see what you are posting online that they can use against you. It is advised that you not discuss the details of your case with anyone except your attorney while the outcome is still pending.

Mistake 12: Giving a Recorded Statement or Signing a Medical Authorization for the Insurance Company.

You do not have to give a recorded statement or sign a medical authorization. Much like a criminal case, anything you say can and will be used against you. My clients are often shocked when they find out they were never required to give a recorded statement. The adjuster may tell you they can't proceed with your claim until you sign certain paperwork. They may tell you it is just part of their procedures or policy, or even that your employer requires it before paying you. There is no law or rule that requires you to give a recorded statement. The insurance company may have this "policy," but it does not mean you are bound by their "policy" or even that the "policy" is enforceable.

If you have already given a recorded statement, do not panic. Call me toll free at 855-760-6746 to discuss the best way to proceed to preserve your legal rights.

CHAPTER SIX

12 THINGS YOU NEED TO KNOW ABOUT INSURANCE COMPANIES

An insurance company is a business and just like any other business, their main goal is to make a profit. The bigger the profit, the better the company performs. Simply put, they have to take in more money than they pay out and ultimately this is what determines just how big their profits will be. While there is nothing wrong with this premise from their standpoint, it does leave you, and your future, vulnerable to their greed. In an effort to achieve their profits, I have noticed FIVE primary traps insurance companies and their adjusters say, and do, hoping that you fall into them.

1. **Believing the insurance adjuster is on your side and is going to treat you fairly**.

After your accident the insurance adjuster who calls you will be pleasant, friendly, and will just want you to answer a few questions so they can help you. Customarily, they will tell you that your medical bills and lost wages are covered and may even offer to pay them as soon as you send them copies. Once received, they will give you one reason or another why the claim cannot be paid and they can't pay your lost wages. This is the first of many false promises and the first of many excuses you will hear. The goal is to get to a quick settlement and prevent you from retaining an attorney.

In other cases they may not want to settle at all. Initially the problem may appear to be something that can easily be remedied by a few actions. Either they will request something else from you or they will state that they need to take care of something additional on their end. However, their primary reason is to stall as long as possible. The

Chapter Six

longer they can stall you, the more likely the Statute of Limitations will run out and you will **never** be able to recoup your medical bills and other expenses for your injury.

2. Believing that you have to give a recorded statement.

When it comes to recorded statements a good rule of thumb is **"anything you say can and will be used against you."** Most people readily admit to their role in their on the job accident because they honestly believe that the insurance adjuster is sincerely trying to help them and understands that the nature of some jobs are dangerous. This is one of the **biggest traps** they hope you fall into. Once they have your version of events they can start building a case against you. If an employee claims they were trying to finish a job that can translate into they were careless and therefor caused their own accident. If they state they were not feeling well at the time of the accident, then the employee should have stayed home.

<u>**You should not give a recorded statement**</u>. As stated in the prior chapter, the adjuster will make an employee believe that a claim can't be processed until they provide a recorded statement. They will also try to convince a worker that it is just part of their procedures or policy. There is no law or rule that requires anyone to give a recorded statement. The insurance company may have this "policy," but it does not mean the worker is bound by their "policy" or that it is even enforceable.

Besides being held to a specific version of events, the adjuster has been trained to ask very specific questions in a very specific way and, most likely, in a very specific order. The same question phrased slightly different can result in two completely different responses. For example, when asked: Do you always wear your safety equipment? A typical response would most likely be a resounding yes.

12 Things You Need to Know About Insurance Companies

However, asked slightly different such as: Have you ever forgotten to wear your safety equipment? The answer might be "on occasion I have" without much hesitation. Not only has the employee just admitted to not abiding by company policy, they have just admitted doing it on multiple occasions. Although this may seem to be an extreme example, I have seen adjusters ask injury victims questions much like this.

I would highly suggest you don't, but the decision to give a recorded statement is entirely up to you.

3. You Do Not Have to Sign a Medical Release or Wage Loss Authorization.

Just as with the recorded statement, the insurance adjuster will likely tell an employee they need to sign a medical authorization form in order to process your claim. Again, an employee need not and should not sign a medical authorization that allows the insurance carrier full access to all medical records. This authorization will give the carrier unlimited access to records relating to prior injuries, pre-existing conditions unrelated to your injuries, illnesses, surgeries, hospitalizations,, medications and all other medical history. Some authorizations even give the defendant's insurance carrier access to your complete educational records or worse; blanket authority to obtain any and all records that can be used against the employee. The insurance company may attempt to use these records to frighten or embarrass a worker into not filing a lawsuit or settling for less than they deserve. They are preying upon the fear that this information will be made public. Please know, they will take every opportunity to exploit any and all information obtained to avoid paying the damages deserved.

Similarly, they usually want a worker to sign a wage loss authorization that may allow the insurance company blanket

Chapter Six

access to all the persons employment records, past and present, including salary, bonuses, any disciplinary actions, reviews, paid time off, and disability information. They will use this information to reduce a claim for lost wages. If an injury was caused at work, obviously they may already have some of this information.

Finally, an employee **SHOULD NOT** sign a check from the insurance company that says *"Final Payment"* or *"Final Settlement."* The insurance companies know if someone falls for this trick, it will be nearly impossible to file a lawsuit at a later date.

4. **The Insurance Company May Not Always Tell You The Truth.**

I have already stated that the insurance companies are in business to make money. Recently, **Fortune Magazine** named insurance companies as one of the top 50 most profitable businesses. Most insurance companies are publicly held. The better they perform, the more valuable their stock becomes, and the larger and more powerful they become.

Don't be fooled into thinking an insurance company, or their agents, and adjusters will tell you the correct answers to your questions. Don't believe they will give an honest estimate of what your injuries are really worth. Finally, don't believe the insurance company is not going to give you what you ask for your injuries if they can pay you less.

5. **Your Injuries Were Pre-Existing and Not Related to Your Accident.**

You can bet if an employee has ever been treated for even a minor injury in the same area of their body, the insurance company will find out and the adjuster will tell them all of their symptoms are due to that prior injury. Most people suffer injuries beginning in early childhood, and periodically throughout their adult life. Therefore, statistically it is quite likely that at some point in the past a person has injured the same area on more than one occasion such as a knee. Don't try to hide a prior injury from the doctors or nurses treating you, or your attorney, because it will give the insurer another reason to avoid paying you. There is nothing harder to deal with in front of a jury than a client caught in a lie about their injuries or how they happened. It is imperative that you are honest and let your attorney determine how best to present your case.

6. **The Insurance Company Does Not Want You to Know the Type of Damages You Are Entitled To.**

Most accident victims already know that they are entitled to compensation for their medical bills and lost wages. The secret the insurance companies are keeping from them is that they are also entitled to recover damages for many other things. Just a few of the more common damages include:

a. **Future Loss of Income** – If an employee's injury results in the loss of income in the future, in any way, they are eligible for future lost wages. This can be due to future treatment or any condition which would impair their earnings in any way. The amount of the damages is equal to the present value of the wages they would have earned during their entire lifetime, if applicable.

b. **Pain and Suffering (Past and Future)** – This term is often familiar to people, but the reasoning behind it is often misunderstood. Sometimes it is viewed as an unnecessary and greedy attempt by an accident victim to get rich from the incident. The value of this element of damages is also not easy to measure. The amount of medical bills is straight forward, but what is the value of the days,

Chapter Six

weeks, or even years of painful healing? In reality, the after effects of an accident are far reaching. Victims and family members can suffer severe, and often, long lasting anguish, fear, depression, and other side effects.

c. **Loss of Useful Life** – An employee is entitled to recover damages for the diminishment in their ability to enjoy and perform the daily activities caused by the accident. This is in addition to, and separate and apart, from pain and suffering. It covers both past and future inability to enjoy life's pleasures including relationships with spouse and children, work, hobbies, driving, housework, gardening and any other activity you could and did do before the incident, but can no longer do or do with added difficulty.

d. **Disfigurement or Amputation** – Scars, loss of limbs, or unsightly marks resulting from an injury entitle the victim to recover damages for the disfigurement, along with the humiliation and embarrassment caused by the disfigurement. In many cases, these damages can be quite substantial. Yet, many victims unknowingly place no value on this, completely unaware that they can recover for their physical scars.

e. **Wrongful Death** - While money can never compensate for the loss of a loved one, it is the only means our system of justice leaves available to compensate the loved ones left behind. Those eligible to recover include; spouses, children, parents, and other relatives, through blood or marriage, who were dependent upon the deceased at the time of the accident. In addition to monetary compensation for the wrongful death of their loved one, survivors may receive damages based on a direct cause of action for injuries to them for loss of companionship, affection, attention, comfort, protection, marital care, parental care, child care, guidance, advice, training, education, mental anguish, and pain and suffering. If the deceased suffered

12 Things You Need to Know About Insurance Companies

prior to their death, their estate may be entitled to damages as well. Under many circumstances this can be very substantial depending on the length of time between the injury and the death of the victim.

7. **Insurance Companies Do Not Want You to Know, or Learn How to Find Out, What Your Injuries are Actually Worth.**

Insurance companies go to great lengths to prevent you from learning how much your injuries are actually worth. The biggest way they do this is to try to prevent you from hiring an attorney. They know that once you do, statistics show you will receive two or three times as much for your injuries. Another way is not to inform you of the resources for valuing your claim. If you are dealing with an adjuster, ask them where you could go to value your claim. I bet they won't direct you to the local jury verdict reporter or a website like mine that will do just that.

8. **The Insurance Company Might Try to Blame You for Your Injuries.**

While an employee may be in part, or in some cases fully, responsible for their injuries this in no way excludes them from receiving full benefits. Many injured workers' wrongfully believe this to be true and therefor may not even seek Workers' Compensation Benefits. If you have been told this by your employer or the insurance company please call me to discuss the details of your case. Your consultation is always FREE. The information you receive may be priceless!

9. **The Insurance Company Does Not Want You to Know the Long Term Consequences of Your Injuries.**

One reason insurance adjusters are often so eager to

Chapter Six

process a claim and offer a quick settlement is to prevent the victim from discovering the extent, and possible long lasting effects, of their injuries. Only you and your doctor can really answer this question and it usually takes time. On the other hand, the insurance companies use a "cookie cutter" technique to assign a value to each injury, or combination of injuries, and assess a dollar amount based on this formula. The Act does assign certain weeks of benefits for loss of limbs and has very specific guidelines. However, it is arrogant on the part of the insurance company, and insulting to you, when they attempt to classify all victims and their injuries into narrowly defined "one-size-fits-all" categories. You are unique, your injuries are unique, and you deserve individualized personal attention to every aspect of your case.

10. The Insurance Company Does Not Want You to Know What a Third-Party Claim is or if One is Available to You.

A third-party claim would involve a set of facts which could make a third-party, someone other than the insurance company's client, responsible for your injuries. These claims often dramatically increase the value of your case. However, if you settle the claim without preserving the 3rd party claim, in some circumstances you may lose this opportunity.

Some examples of third-party claims are:
   a. Accidents caused by faulty equipment or manufactured products.
   b. Injuries caused by an employee of another company at your job site.
   c. Injuries as a result of unsafe premises when owned or operated by someone other than your employer.
   d. Car accidents caused by someone else's negligence when you are driving as part of your job.

12 Things You Need to Know About Insurance Companies

If you are not aware that you can file a claim against a third-party, in almost all cases, the insurance company is not going to tell you. If you think someone else may be liable for your injuries, I highly recommend you call me to discuss how it may affect your claim.

11. The Insurance Company Does Not Want You to Know That Accident Victims Receive 2-3 Times More Money With an Attorney.

Victims represented by an attorney typically receive two to three times more money than they obtain when they represent themselves. Insurance companies ***don't want*** you to know this. If you are dealing with an adjuster, ask him if they would advise you to speak to an attorney before proceeding any further. I bet you will hear a lot of things, but one thing you won't hear is "yes, I suggest you seek legal counsel immediately." This is why the insurance companies want to settle your claim quickly and why the adjuster will do everything possible to keep you from hiring a lawyer.

In Illinois, statistics show that the average settlement for an auto accident in 2010 was a little over $30,000 if the individual was not represented by an attorney and between $60,000 and $90,000 for the same damages if they were represented by an attorney. However, small accidents, typically under $5,000 in damages, may not require the assistance of an experienced personal injury attorney. You still should know what to expect when dealing with a potentially unscrupulous insurance adjuster. Therefore, it is always a good idea to call me for a free, no obligation case analysis and just get some good, honest advice on what to do and what the settlement value of your case likely is given your injuries.

Chapter Six

12. The Insurance Company Will Look for Many Reasons to Deny Your Claim, Hoping You Won't Challenge Them.

Insurance companies will sometimes give you multiple or repeated reasons why you are not eligible for certain benefits. Some of the more common ones are that you did not go to the correct doctor for your particular injuries and will therefore try to deny coverage to certain types of doctors including, but not limited to, chiropractors, plastic surgeons, and orthodontists. Additionally, they will argue certain treatments were unnecessary or excessive, even if prescribed as part of your overall recovery plan. Then there will be facilities they try to exclude too. Sport medicine clinics routinely perform physical therapy, yet the insurance company will claim your injury does not qualify you to be seen there or that you were over treated. The insurance company tries to inject itself into the doctor-patient relationship and dictate treatment. They have no business here, but a trained attorney is needed to deal with these issues

CHAPTER SEVEN

CHOOSING THE RIGHT WORKERS' COMPENSATION ATTORNEY

Getting injured at work is traumatic and can be very anxiety provoking, especially if the injured worker is the primary provider for the family. In addition to your injuries there is the stress of dealing with how you will provide for your family, pay the medical bills or you may be worried about losing your job if you file a worker's compensation claim.

Your main objective is to get well and return to the workforce and the stress of trying to handle your claim on your own may actually complicate or hinder your recovery. Illinois worker's compensation cases are very complex and can get extremely technical as the employer will bring in their experts to testify against you. Unfamiliar terms such as "MMI," "TTD benefits," "PPD benefits," "19-B petition," "section 16(k) penalties," and "8(d)(1) case will be used throughout the hearing by the insurance company's attorney as a tactic to intimidate you and keep you from arguing against their findings. An experienced and qualified attorney will not only speak the same "language," they will be able to spot the issues that will maximize your recovery while minimizing the deficiencies in your case.

How will you know the right attorney for you and your case? They all say they are the best or something to that effect. You need to get to the right lawyer and sort out the bad ones quickly.

To assist you in getting through this process, I have found that most people face the following issues shortly after being injured;

1. **Do I need to hire an attorney to represent me in this case?**

Chapter Seven

2. **How do I determine the right attorney for my case?**
3. **Family, friends, or others have recommended an attorney. How do I know if he or she is right for me?**

No matter which way you go, you should start the process as soon as possible after the accident. This usually means within days, or at least the first few weeks, depending on your injuries. You can rest assured that your employer's insurance company has a team of people working on the case in an attempt to reduce the amount they will have to pay you in the end.

Do I need an attorney to represent me? I recommend that, in almost all cases, it is a good idea to obtain the advice of an attorney. Often times I recommend to individuals that they handle the case themselves. We live in a society where all too many people are sue happy. Although I advocate that people should be properly compensated for their injuries, I do not advocate the filing of lawsuits based on frivolous claims or the refusal to settle minor incidents with insurance companies who are offering reasonable settlements. If your case involves a significant amount of medical bills, lost wages, and other damages, it is likely that hiring an attorney will substantially benefit you in the end.

Before making this decision, it is important to understand how a workers' compensation attorney is compensated. Although many people have a general idea about this, most people do not understand the details contained in the Workers' Compensation attorney/client contract. The contract is based on a contingency fee and ALL WORKERS' COMPENSATION CONTRACTS ARE THE SAME. Contingency means the attorney is compensated based on a percentage of the settlement or judgment that is received in the case. The percentage is generally fixed at 20%. If you have received a written offer from the insurance company the attorney is limited to 40% of the increased award. The 20%, or 40%, as the case may be, is only of the PPD benefits

Choosing the Right Workers' Compensation Attorney

generally plus any other disputed benefits. The attorney is not compensated for the TTD or medical bills unless the employer disputes them.

The best answer to the question of whether or not to hire a lawyer is to contact an experienced attorney and seek advice as to whether or not they recommend you retain legal counsel for your particular situation. I invite you to contact me for a free, honest evaluation of your case. Again, often times I recommend that people handle a case themselves and give them a substantial amount of advice and information on just how to do it. You are always welcome to contact my firm to seek advice on the best course of action for your given circumstances.

How do I select the right attorney for my case? Although there are many criteria to consider in the selection of an attorney, probably the most important are experience with cases of your type, a proven long track record of success, and testimonials from people just like yourself giving you assurance that you will be satisfied throughout the process. Client testimonials can be viewed directly on my website at www.RobertEdensLawOffice.com and new ones are continually being added.

I have over 20 years of legal experience representing thousands of injured workers'. It is important that you select an attorney that can take your case to the end. Not only have I represented thousands of injured victims, but I have tried hundreds of cases both in front of juries and judges, as well as taken many cases to winning appeals. I am known for my aggressive, no nonsense, approach to insurance pre-litigation negotiations. Once a complaint is filed, I will use a streamlined and fast tracked method of getting the case settled or achieving judgment through a hearing.

My legal team is experienced at gathering evidence and using the latest technology to strongly persuade the insurance companies to give you the money you deserve.

Chapter Seven

Everyone at my firm knows how the legal game is played and will be here to help you with everything from answering questions to preparing you for a hearing if necessary.

It is through my years of experience, knowledge of evidence and technology, along with my relationships with the players in the insurance field that has earned me the reputation as a top notch negotiator and the leading workers' compensation attorney throughout Northern Illinois.

As soon as I become involved in your case, myself and my team will immediately begin the process of gathering evidence to support your claim. This will include obtaining medical records, doctor's notes, narratives, accident reports, and accident reconstruction, if required. It does not matter whether you were injured by faulty equipment or even your own negligence, you need to immediately gather and preserve the evidence necessary to secure your worker's rights. I have handled cases involving wrongful death, catastrophic injuries, premises liability, product liability, and many others. I have the resources necessary to pursue your claim and level the playing field between you and your employer's insurance company.

Family, friends or others have suggested an attorney; how do I know if he or she is right for me? I am often called by individuals who have been referred by family, friends, or others. Unlike many other attorneys, I will be the first to admit when I am not the right attorney to handle your case and whenever possible, I will recommend an attorney who is. It bothers me greatly when a lawyer is asked if they will accept a workers' compensation case and they agree to do so even if they have little or no experience in the field. By doing this, they are doing themselves, and their clients, a great disservice. I have been asked by many clients to aid them in their legal issues regarding copyright infringement, bankruptcy issues, contract issues, and real estate issues. All areas are outside my field. The best I can do is refer a

Choosing the Right Workers' Compensation Attorney

competent attorney that I know who practices in the area or tell them how to find one.

How then do you know if the attorney you are calling is right for you? The first thing you can do is ask questions such as, how much of the practice is devoted to workers' compensation? Do they have a website you could review? Have they written and published any books or other materials in the field of workers' compensation? How many cases of your type has the practice handled? How many workers' compensation hearings has he/she done? Has the attorney ever done appellate work? Do they have client testimonials relating to workers' compensation cases? What kind of settlements have they received? How many attorneys work at their firm? Each of these questions will help you decide on the right attorney to handle your case.

With regard to the last question, often times it may seem that firms with a large number of attorneys are beneficial. However, the answer to this may be just the opposite because in today's economy many of the large firms are finding it more and more difficult to maintain the high cost of high priced lawyer salaries and as a result they are taking on more and more cases of a smaller size than they had in prior years. Then the smaller cases get buried in a pile on an associate's desk at the firm, getting little or no attention. Don't let your case become a victim to this type of large law firm. Your case deserves personal, individualized, attention.

If you select The Law Offices of Robert T. Edens, I will personally handle your case, giving it the attention it requires for a successful outcome. When you call my office, not only will the phone be answered by someone who knows you personally, but also knows the status of your case. We pride ourselves on client communications; keeping our clients abreast of where their case stands at all times. If at any time you can't reach me personally, because I am

Chapter Seven

conducting a trial or with another client, my staff, who knows you personally, will be able to assist you.

Not only will you always be informed of the status of your case and its current progress, you will be kept informed of any negotiations with the insurance company and any offers made on your case will be conveyed to you as soon as they are made, often the same day. If your case can't be settled favorably, you will know well in advance and be thoroughly prepared by my team of experts before going to a hearing. No settlement will ever be made on your case without your authority. I will make it clear and you will understand exactly what costs will be incurred on your behalf and how they will impact your case. No rock will go unturned in an effort to maximize the amount of money you get for your injury.

I have handled cases involving brain injuries, loss of limbs and catastrophic injuries. I have extensive experience with injuries to the back, neck, knees, hips, wrists, shoulders, ankle injuries, and many more. It is not only important that your attorney have experience with the type of injury, he/she must be experienced in anticipating what the insurance company's position will be and what maneuvers they will use in an attempt to devalue your case. Most workers' compensation cases involve a battle of the experts. This means that your treating physicians will be testifying concerning your injuries and the cause of those injuries and they are experts in medicine, not law. On the other hand, the insurance company will hire an outside doctor who routinely testifies on their behalf, reporting on the nature of your injuries and whether or not they were caused by the incident involved. It is this expert testimony that requires a seasoned attorney with knowledge of your particular injury and how to counter the defense's expert opposition.

CHAPTER EIGHT

PREPARING YOUR WORKERS' COMPENSATION CASE

Once you have hired The Law Offices of Robert T. Edens work on your case begins immediately.

With your assistance, I will review the facts of your case in order to give you an honest assessment of the value of your case. I will review any accident reports, photos, medical records, insurance documents, and any other paperwork you have. Afterwards, I will give you an overall assessment of your case including your chances of recovery.

A more in-depth evaluation will take place once all documents pertaining to your work-place injury have been obtained. This will include current and prior medical records, doctor's notes and narrative reports, accident reports, and everything else needed to evaluate your case; then I will explain to you the entire process from start to finish as it applies to your case.

Depending on what you and I agree is the best approach, myself and my staff will prepare a demand on your employer including detailed support on liability, as well as case value. Again, this will often include other verdict studies, medical opinions, accident reconstructions, day-in-the-life videos, future care plans and whatever else is necessary to fully prepare this demand.

FREQUENTLY ASKED QUESTIONS

The question every client wants to know is "what is my case worth?"

Any experienced attorney will tell you there is no way to determine that until all treatment has been completed and you have been released from your doctor's care. Valuing a claim is not an exact science. It will vary depending on your medical bills, lost wages, long-term prognosis, pain and suffering, and so on. You can view recent case results at www.RobertEdensLawOffice.com to get an idea of what your case might be worth.

How can I afford to hire the best attorney?

Almost without exception, I work on a contingency basis and pay all costs associated with your claim. You will know exactly what my fees are and how they are determined in advance. If no recovery is made, you owe me nothing. It is not until after your case is settled or you received a judgment that you will pay the costs associated with prosecuting your claim. You will be provided a detailed expense sheet showing all amounts spent on your behalf. With no risk, there is no reason you should not hire the best attorney and concentrate on getting well.

How long do I have to file a claim?

<u>I can't say this enough; it is critical that you do not let the statute of limitations pass</u>. Generally, you have 3 years from the date of your injury or two years from the last payment of benefits, whichever is later. This is the statutory time frame allowed and once it passes you will be forever barred from receiving further benefits

How long will it take to receive any money?

This depends on whether your case is settled or goes to a hearing. In either situation, you most likely will not receive your PPD until you have fully recovered from your injuries, or until, with reasonable certainty, your treating physician can estimate the future cost of your medical expenses. If you settle your case and sign a release, you will be forever barred from seeking damages relating to that incident. Therefore, it is in your best interest to wait until you injuries are fully known.

Will I have to go to court?

If a satisfactory settlement can be reached, you will have to have a hearing on your claim for adjustment. You will typically need to give a sworn statement. During the statement you will be asked questions about the accident, your injuries, and your treatment. The only time you will usually go to court is for the hearing or a pre-trial with the hearing officer. A pre-trial is a conference with the hearing officer where the parties explain their case and the officer helps them to settle the matter without a hearing.

CONCLUSION

It is my sincere hope that this book has opened your eyes to many of the tactics used by insurance companies to reduce the amount they have to pay legitimate claims and much, much, more. You may have already decided whether or not you need to hire a lawyer. Not everyone does, but if you need the assistance of a skillful, experienced, workers' compensation attorney I invite you to contact me personally at my toll free number (855)760-6746 or through my website, www.RobertEdensLawOffice.com to schedule a free, no pressure, consultation were I will give you my honest opinion on the value of your case. The call is free, the advice might be priceless.

DONT'T FAIL TO ACT AND LET THE STATUTE OF LIMITATION EXPIRE!

To learn more about me, our firm, actual settlements, awards and verdicts please visit my website at www.RobertEdensLawOffice.com. While there, I invite you to review testimonials from my clients who have considerately and voluntarily given them.

NOTES

NOTES

www.ingramcontent.com/pod-product-compliance
Lightning Source LLC
Chambersburg PA
CBHW071804170526
45167CB00003B/1164